Oratory and Democracy in China: four dialogues from the *Annals of the Warring States*

Translated by Mingyuan Hu

Hermits United
London · Paris

Published in Great Britain by Hermits United Ltd. 2022
English translation copyright © Mingyuan Hu 2022
Second Printing 2023. Printed in Europe

This book is part of the Erstwhile Series
A catalogue record for this book is available
from the British Library
ISBN 978-1-7391156-0-9

www.hermits-united.com

Oratory and Democracy in China

475–221 BC

Written by diverse and anonymous authors, the *Annals of the Warring States* records the School of Diplomacy at work during one of the most captivating times in Chinese history. In four dialogues, selected and translated by Mingyuan Hu, thinking beings challenge sovereign power in ways that surprise and resonate. They make visible an astonishing relationship between politics and the intellect, and echo our notions of oratory and democracy in differing contexts.

| 鄒忌諷齊王納諫 | 11 |
| Zou Ji Advising the King of Qi to Invite Counsel | 15 |

| 顏斶說齊王 | 22 |
| Yan Chu Persuading the King of Qi | 29 |

| 趙威后問齊使 | 43 |
| Dowager Queen Wei of Zhao Questioning the Ambassador of Qi | 46 |

| 唐雎不辱使命 | 52 |
| Tang Ju Accomplishing His Mission | 56 |

鄒忌諷齊王納諫

鄒忌修八尺有餘、而形貌昳麗。朝服衣冠窺鏡、謂其妻曰、我孰與城北徐公美。其妻曰、君美甚、徐公何能及君也。城北徐公、齊國之美麗者也。忌不自信、而復問其妾曰、吾孰與徐公美。妾曰、徐公何能及君也。旦日、客從外來、與坐談、問之客曰、吾與徐公孰美。客曰、徐公不若君之美也。明日徐公來、孰視之、自以為不如。窺鏡而自視、又弗如遠甚。暮寢而思之、曰、吾妻之美我者、私我也、妾之

美我者、畏我也、客之美我者、欲
有求於我也。於是入朝見威王、
曰、臣誠知不如徐公美。臣之妻私
臣、臣之妾畏臣、臣之客欲有求於
臣、皆以美於徐公。今齊地方千
里、百二十城、宮婦左右莫不私
王、朝廷之臣莫不畏王、四境之內
莫不有求於王、由此觀之、王之蔽
甚矣。王曰、善。乃下令、羣臣吏
民、能面刺寡人之過者、受上賞、
上書諫寡人者、受中賞、能謗譏於
市朝、聞寡人之耳者、受下賞。令

初下、羣臣進諫、門庭若市。數月之後、時時而間進。期年之後、雖欲言、無可進者。燕、趙、韓、魏聞之、皆朝於齊。此所謂戰勝於朝廷。

Zou Ji Advising the King of Qi to Invite Counsel

Zou Ji, standing two metres tall, was radiantly handsome. Dressing in the morning, looking into the mirror, he asked his wife: 'Who is the more handsome, Sir Xu of City North or I?' His wife replied: 'You are so handsome. How can Sir Xu compare?' Sir Xu of City North was a most handsome man of the State of Qi. Unsure, Ji asked his concubine: 'Who is the more handsome, Sir Xu or I?' His concubine replied: 'How can Sir Xu compare?' The following day, a guest came to visit. Sitting and conversing with him, Ji asked: 'Who is the more handsome, Sir Xu or I?' The guest replied: 'Sir Xu cannot compare in handsomeness.'

The following day, Sir Xu came over. Ji regarded him intently, and thought himself inferior; looking later into the mirror, he considered himself a long way off. That night, lying in bed he reflected: 'My wife judges me more handsome, for she prefers me. The concubine judges me more handsome, for she fears me. The guest judges me more handsome, for he wants something from me.'

Wherefore he went to see King Wei of Qi. 'I know myself in all honesty to be less handsome than Sir Xu,' he said. 'My wife prefers me; my concubine fears me; my guest wants something from me. They all judge me more handsome than Sir Xu. Now the State of Qi has thousands of *li* of land and a hundred and twenty cities. Women in the palace all prefer our King. Ministers in the court all fear our King. Everyone in the state wants something from our King. Ergo, our King must be most removed from reality.'

'Fine,' said the King. He then gave the order: 'Officials and citizens, he who tells the benighted of his fault in person shall receive a large reward; he who writes to advise the benighted shall receive a medium reward; he who criticises the benighted in public and whose criticism reaches the ears of the benighted shall receive a small reward.'

Shortly after the announcement, statesmen crowded into the court to present advice. Months later, from time to time they came forward. A year later, even with the desire to exhort, they had nothing more to suggest.

The Kings of Yan, Zhao, Han and Wei heard about this. They all paid tribute to the King of Qi. Such was the victory at court.

顏斶說齊王

齊宣王見顏斶、曰、斶前。斶亦曰、王前。宣王不説。左右曰、王、人君也、斶、人臣也。王曰斶前、斶亦曰王前、可乎。斶對曰、夫斶前為慕勢、王前為趨士。與使斶為慕勢、不如使王為趨士。王忿然作色曰、王者貴乎、士貴乎。對曰、士貴耳、王者不貴。王曰、有説乎。斶曰、有。昔者秦攻齊、令曰、有敢去柳下季壟五十步而樵採者、死不赦。令曰、有能得齊王頭者、封萬戶侯、賜金千鎰。由是

觀之、生王之頭、曾不若死士之壟
也。宣王默然不悅。左右皆曰、斶
來，斶來。大王據千乘之地、而建
千石鍾、萬石虡。天下之士、仁義
皆來役處。辯士並進、莫不來語。
東西南北、莫敢不服。求萬物無不
備具、而百姓無不親附。今夫士之
高者、乃稱匹夫、徒步而處農畝、
下則鄙野、監門、閭里。士之賤
也、亦甚矣。斶對曰、不然。斶聞
古大禹之時、諸侯萬國。何則。德
厚之道、得貴士之力也。故舜起農

畝、出於嶽鄙、而為天子。及湯之時、諸侯三千。當今之世、南面稱寡者、乃二十四。由此觀之、非得失之策與。稍稍誅滅、滅亡無族之時、欲為監門、閭里、安可得而有乎哉。是故易傳不云乎、居上位、未得其實、以喜其為名者、必以驕奢為行。據慢驕奢、則兇從之。是故無其實而喜其名者削、無德而望其福者約、無功而受其祿者辱、禍必握。故曰、矜功不立、虛願不至。此皆幸樂其名、華而無其實德者也。是以堯有九佐、舜有七友、禹有五丞、湯有三輔、自古及今而能虛成名於天下者、無有。是以君王無羞亟問、不愧下學。是故成其道德而揚功名於後世者、堯、舜、禹、湯、周文王是也。故曰、無形者、形之君也。無端者、事之本也。夫上見其原、下通其流、至聖人明學、何不吉之有哉。老子曰、雖貴、必以賤為本。雖高、必以下為基。是以侯王稱孤寡不穀、是其賤必本於。非夫孤寡者、人之困賤

下位也、而侯王以自謂、豈非下人
而尊貴士與。夫堯傳舜、舜傳禹、
周成王任周公旦、而世世稱曰明
主、是以明乎士之貴也。宣王曰、
嗟乎、君子焉可侮哉、寡人自取病
耳。及今聞君子之言、乃今聞細人
之行、願請受為弟子。且顏先生與
寡人遊、食必太牢、出必乘車、妻
子衣服麗都。顏斶辭去曰、夫玉生
於山、制則破焉、非弗寶貴矣、然
夫璞不完。士生乎鄙野、推選則祿
焉、非不得尊遂也、然而形神不

全。觸願得歸、晚食以當肉、安步以當車、無罪以當貴、清靜貞正以自虞。制言者王也、盡忠直言者觸也。言要道已備矣、願得賜歸、安行而反臣之邑屋。則再拜而辭去也。君子曰、觸知足矣、歸真返璞、則終身不辱。

Yan Chu
Persuading
the King of Qi

Receiving Yan Chu, King Xuan of Qi said: 'Come forward, Chu!' Chu said: 'Come forward, King!' King Xuan was displeased. The courtiers said: 'The King is our sovereign. Chu is the servant. When the King asked Chu to come forward, Chu asked the King to come forward. Is this appropriate?' Chu replied: 'Coming forward, Chu would be desirous of power. Coming forward, the King would be reverent toward the scholar. Rather than a Chu desirous of power, a king reverent toward the scholar is better.' The King, visibly irate, said: 'Is the King eminent? Is the scholar eminent?' Chu replied: 'The scholar is eminent. The King is not.' The King said: 'Do you have an argument?' Chu said: 'I do. In the old days, when the King of Qin attacked the State of Qi, he ordered: "He who dares cut wood within fifty steps of Liuxia Hui's tomb shall be executed without mercy." He also announced: "He who beheads the King of Qi shall be made a marquess and rewarded thousands of *yi* of gold." Seen from this point of view, a living king's head was once worth less than a dead scholar's tomb.' King Xuan brooded in silence.

The courtiers all said: 'Come over, Chu, come over! Our King has a territory of a thousand chariots and builds bells weighing thousands of *shi* and bell-stands weighing tens of thousands. Talents from everywhere are here to serve. Orators and sophists alike arrive with things to say. All states obey our King. Anything our King wants, he has, not least the support of all people. The most elevated scholars of our day are ordinary, farming footmen doing small jobs in obscure places. The lowliness of scholars is quite something!'

Chu retorted: 'Not true. Chu has heard that, in the ancient times of King Yu, there were tens of thousands of marquesses with their own states. Why? Yu was virtuous; for that reason, he had the help of eminent scholars. For the same reason, Shun, a peasant, became King of all states. Later under the reign of Tang, there were three thousand marquesses. Now in our day, twenty-four marquesses call themselves "the benighted". Seen from this point of view, is the difference not a matter of "gain" or "loss" of scholars? Little by little, marquesses have been killed and their clans destroyed. Even becoming a lowly guardian or janitor has become difficult. As is said in the *I Ching* commentaries: "Occupying a high position but possessing no moral substance, those interested in vain fame can act only in arrogance and extravagance. Their arrogance and extravagance will be their downfall: thence, he who has not the substance but likes the appearance, his power will diminish; he who has no morals but desires good fortune, his luck will lessen; he who has no achievements but takes the benefits will end up in disgrace. All this brings misfortune." Hence the saying: "Opportunists accomplish nothing. Vain dreamers fulfil no dreams." They are shallow hedonists without actual virtue. That is why King Yao had nine counsels, King Shun had seven friends, King Yu had five ministers, and King Tang had three aides. Since time immemorial, great names made without concrete deeds do not exist. Thus, kings have no shame in consulting or learning from others. Thus, virtuous men with an enduring reputation are King Yao, King Shun, King Yu, King Tang, and King Wen of Zhou. Thus, it is said: "The formless governs form; the sourceless is the source of all." He who understands both the outset and the evolution of things attains the wisdom of the saints, and, so doing, how can he not be blessed? Lao Tse said: "The noble has as its base the humble. The high has as its foundation the low. Thence, marquesses and kings speak of themselves as 'the forsaken' and 'the benighted'. They seek humility as base." The forsaken and the benighted assume a lowly position. When marquesses and kings call themselves such, is it not an argument for venerating scholars? King Yao made Shun his successor, King Shun made Yu his successor, and King Cheng of Zhou appointed Duke Wen of Zhou. Generation after generation has considered these men to be enlightened sovereigns, for they were enlightened about the eminence of scholars.'

King Xuan sighed: 'Ah! How can a superior man be humiliated? The benighted deserves to be belittled! Hearing a superior man speak today, the benighted sees his own acts as a petty man, and asks to be the superior man's disciple. If Master Yan would work with the benighted, he would feast on delicacies and travel in carriages; his wife and children would wear attires most stylish.'

Yan Chu declined the offer: 'Originating in the mountains, the jade is broken when made into jewellery. Not that the jewellery is not precious, but the jade's wholeness is lost. Born an outsider, a scholar becomes a functionary when commended to the court. Not that he is not revered, but his heart and soul's wholeness is lost. Chu would like to return, to eat late as his delicacies, take a stroll as his carriage, be a lawful citizen as his eminence, and stay upright as his joy. The one who gives orders is the King. The one who loyally speaks truth to the King is Chu. I have said what I have to say. Now I wish to be granted my return to my humble abode.' Bowing twice, he took his leave.

The superior men say: 'Chu was content with what he had. Returning to his wholeness, he shunned indignity for the rest of his life.'

趙威后問齊使

齊王使使者問趙威后。書未發、威后問使者曰、歲亦無恙耶、民亦無恙耶、王亦無恙耶。使者不說、曰、臣奉使使威后、今不問王、而先問歲與民、豈先賤而後尊貴者乎。威后曰、不然。苟無歲、何以有民、苟無民、何以有君。故有問。捨本而問末者耶。乃進而問之曰、齊有處士曰鍾離子、無恙耶。是其為人也、有糧者亦食、無糧者亦食、有衣者亦衣、無衣者亦衣。是助王養其民也、何以至今不業也。葉陽子無恙乎。是其為人、哀鰥寡、恤孤獨、振困窮、補不足。是助王息其民者也、何以至今不業也。北宮之女嬰兒子無恙耶。徹其環瑱、至老不嫁、以養父母。是皆率民而出於孝情者也、胡為至今不朝也。此二士弗業、一女不朝、何以王齊國、子萬民乎。於陵子仲尚存乎。是其為人也、上不臣於王、下不治其家、中不索交諸侯。此率民而出於無用者、何為至今不殺乎。

Dowager Queen Wei of Zhao
Questioning
the Ambassador of Qi

The King of Qi sent an ambassador to greet Dowager Queen Wei of Zhao. Before opening the King's letter, Queen Wei asked the ambassador: 'How is the harvest? How are the people? How is the King?'

Dismayed, the ambassador said: 'I have been sent to greet Queen Wei. Rather than asking after our King, she first asks about the harvest and the people. Is this putting the humble before the noble?'

Queen Wei said: 'Not so. Without the harvest, where stand the people? Without the people, where stands the King? Hence the question. Ought one to have begun with not the paramount but the consequent?'

Further she asked: 'There is, in the State of Qi, a gentleman without a political function named Zhongli. How is he? When it comes to his comportment, he gives food equally to those with and without food and gives clothing equally to those with and without clothing. He is helping the King nourish his people. Why is he still not ennobled? How is Sheyang? When it comes to his comportment, he sympathises with those widowed or unmarried in old age; mourns with those who have lost their parents or their children; provides for those in poverty; supports those struggling to make ends meet. He is someone who helps the King comfort his people. Why is he still not ennobled? The daughter of Beigong, by the name of Yingerzi, how is she? Renouncing wearing her jewellery, she has stayed unmarried to care for her parents. Here is an exemplar leading the people in filial piety. Why is she still not honoured? With these two men not ennobled and this one woman not honoured, with what does the King govern the State of Qi and nurture his people? Zizhong from Wuling, is he still alive? When it comes to his comportment, he does not serve the kings, does not manage his family, and does not take up with the marquesses. This is someone who encourages the people to be idle. Why has he still not been killed?'

唐雎不辱使命

秦王使人謂安陵君曰、寡人欲以五百里之地易安陵、安陵君其許寡人。安陵君曰、大王加惠、以大易小、甚善。雖然、受地於先王、願終守之、弗敢易。秦王不説。安陵君因使唐雎使於秦。秦王謂唐雎曰、寡人慾以五百里之地易安陵、安陵君不聽寡人、何也。且秦滅韓亡魏、而君以五十里之地存者、以君為長者、故不錯意也。今吾以十倍之地、請廣於君、而君逆寡人者、輕寡人與。唐雎對曰、否、非若是也。安陵君受地於先王而守之、雖千里不敢易也、豈直五百里哉。秦王怫然怒、謂唐雎曰、公亦嘗聞天子之怒乎。唐雎對曰、臣未嘗聞也。秦王曰、天子之怒、伏屍百萬、流血千里。唐雎曰、大王嘗聞布衣之怒乎。秦王曰、布衣之怒、亦免冠徒跣、以頭搶地耳。唐雎曰、此庸夫之怒也、非士之怒也。夫專諸之刺王僚也、彗星襲月。聶政之刺韓傀也、白虹貫日。要離之刺慶忌也、倉鷹擊於殿上。

此三子者、皆布衣之士也、懷怒未發、休祲降於天、與臣而將四矣。若士必怒、伏屍二人、流血五步、天下縞素、今日是也。挺劍而起。秦王色撓、長跪而謝之曰、先生坐、何至於此。寡人諭矣、夫韓、魏滅亡、而安陵以五十里之地存者、徒以有先生也。

Tang Ju
Accomplishing
His Mission

The King of Qin sent a message to the Duke of Anling: 'The benighted wishes to give a territory of five hundred *li* in exchange for Anling. The Duke of Anling will grant the benighted his wish!'

The Duke of Anling said: 'The King is generous. Bestowing something large in exchange for something small, he is kind indeed. That said, having received my territory from the former King, I would like to keep it to the end, and dare not exchange it.'

The King of Qin was not pleased. The Duke of Anling therefore sent Tang Ju to visit Qin.

The King of Qin said to Tang Ju: 'The benighted wishes to give a land of five hundred *li* in exchange for Anling. The Duke of Anling does not grant the benighted his wish. Why? Qin has, moreover, conquered Han and Wei; the Duke's fifty *li* is intact, for I appreciate the elderly Duke and do not mean him harm.

Now I hand out ten times more land for the Duke to expand his territory, yet the Duke goes against the benighted. Does he look down on the benighted?'

Tang Ju replied: 'No, such is not the case. The Duke of Anling keeps his land received from the former King. He dares not exchange it even for one thousand *li*, let alone five hundred.'

Flying into a rage, the King of Qin asked Tang Ju: 'Sir, have you ever heard of the rage of a sovereign?' Tang Ju replied: 'I haven't.' The King said: 'The rage of a sovereign results in millions of corpses and thousands of *li* of bloodshed.'

Tang Ju said: 'Has the King ever heard of the rage of a commoner?' The King said: 'The rage of a commoner manifests merely in throwing off the hat and shoes and bashing the head against the ground.'

Tang Ju said: 'Such is the rage

of a mediocre man, not the rage of an honourable gentleman. The day Zhuan Zhu slew King Liao of Wu, a comet hit the moon. The day Nie Zheng slew Han Gui, a moonbow pierced the sun. The day Yao Li slew Qing Ji, an eagle attacked the temple. All three were commoners. Before their rage was manifested, heaven had presaged it. Counting me, there will now be four. The rage of a gentleman results in two corpses, five strides of bloodshed, and funeral garments everywhere under heaven. And that is now.' Drawing his sword, Tang Ju rose.

The King of Qin changed colour. Sitting up, he apologised: 'Sir, please take a seat. We are not there. The benighted understands: Han and Wei having perished, Anling survives with a territory of fifty *li* because of you, Sir.'